ON THE
LITE-R
SIDE

Fat-Free Inspiration

Barbour Books, Westwood, New Jersey

MW01614296

Published by **Barbour and Company, Inc., P.O. Box 1219, Westwood, New Jersey 07675.**

Typesetting by Typetronix, Inc., Cape Coral, Florida

ISBN 1-55748-253-5

Printed in the United States of America

1 2 3 4 5/ 96 95 94 93 92 91

If instead of a gem, or even a flower, we could cast the gift of a lovely thought into the heart of a friend, that would be giving as the angels give.

GEORGE MacDONALD

God will not leave us when we respond to His call!

We are not alone in our attempt to lose weight!

Dieting can draw me closer to being a disciple!

God's bread of life is nonfattening!

The reward of our diet is greater than the sacrifice!

We always look better in God's light than in our own darkness.

God wants to see us achieve our goal!

Let us learn from the sacrifice of Christ and remember that He has given us the power to overcome any temptation that might present itself. Christ has conquered temptation and will be with me!

Talk to Jesus. Seriously, He is waiting to listen to you and help you in your struggle to lose weight. Jesus is as close as a prayer!

Each pound lost cleanses me physically, spiritually, and mentally.

If we see ourselves as overweight,
we will tend to think less of ourselves.
There's a brand new me on the way!

I am facing nothing that Christ did not face before me.

There are ways to be fed (spiritually) without getting fat!

I must set my mind on more important things than food!

Losing one battle doesn't mean I've lost the war!

I will put far away anything that tempts me this day!

When my diet gets toughest, God will be closest.

There's no such thing as cheating just a little!

Jesus knows that we sometimes give in, and He loves us just the same.

Christ is better than any diet book!

But know this: God will make sure we can hang on, if we include Him in our diet attempts.

No matter how lonely I might feel,
Jesus is right beside me!

Dieting makes me a spiritual overcomer as well as a physical overcomer!

Fat is the enemy. We have declared the war, and it takes every ounce of strength we have to wage the battle.

When we can forgive and forget, we stand a much better chance of a successful diet.

Any attempt I make to lose weight
is incomplete without God!

As the fat fades, so does the tribulation!

Food wasted is better than food waisted!

The more time spent in prayer, the less time left to eat!

I will think of what I have, rather than what I have not!

As we cast our cares on God, He casts His love on us!

God is not the source of temptation, just the solution!

Knowing our limits helps us limit our wants!

To diet means to do it!

When I look my best, I look most like Christ!

I'm not letting my stomach push me around anymore!

I will let my hunger turn my mind to God!

God makes me fit to fight fat!

God is all the pick-me-up I need!

Jesus will take my mind off my diet!

If I can make it through the tough times, I can make it through anything!

I am the nonfattening apple of God's eye!

I'll prove to all my skeptical friends that I am capable of losing weight.

All else fails; try God!

I will rejoice at the example of others who have lost weight!

I may lose weight, but I can't lose God.

Even dieters deserve a day off.

When my stomach attacks, God will defend me!

Thank you Lord, for bringing me this far!

The longer the wait, the less the weight!

I can take this diet one day at a time!

Beware skinny people with fat mouths!

Lord, make me ready to lose weight!

Losing weight is no excuse for losing patience!

If I keep my mouth shut, food can't get in!

Filling up with the Holy Spirit satisfies, and it isn't fattening!

I'd rather put on patience than put on weight!

I will make a little last a long, long time!

There's more to a new me than just losing weight.

This day means I am one day closer to the end of my diet!

There are a lot of things more inter-
esting than food!

The busier I keep myself, the thinner I get!

I want my life to be much more than food and drink!

Chocolate cake is nothing but devil's food!

I can suffer today for a new me tomorrow!

If it is my heart's desire to be thin,
God will help me!

As the wait goes on, the weight comes off!

A new me is mine for the asking!

God believes in me!

Following fads is frustrating and foolish!

Trust is a must for weight to abate!

I am made stronger every day that I diet!

If I can remove mountains, then I can remove pounds!

I will turn to Jesus whenever I need a faith lift!

Help me to benefit from the faith of others!

God is bigger than any craving my mind and stomach can come up with!

Thank God for the gift of determination!

In dieting, the biggest winner is the biggest loser!

I need God's help to ask for the right things.

Watch me closely Lord, I'm hungry,
and I'm weak.

Let my spirit be immovable, not my body!

Let me be a *little* child of God!

The same power that withers figs can wither fat!

Oh, Lord, please protect me from me!

I'm proud of what I'm trying to do!

I'm not dying of hunger; it just feels that way!

I'm better than I was yesterday, and I can't wait until tomorrow!

No matter is too insignificant to bring to God!

What I lose today in weight will be gain in other ways tomorrow!

Dieting is more than a matter of the mind. It's a matter of the heart!

Christ helps those who choose to be different!

God gives us hope in order to cope!

I'm keeping God between me and the refrigerator!

I am one of God's miracles, and He will help me be my best!

When we aren't tough enough on ourselves, God will be as tough as we need Him to be!

God's might is greater than my appetite!

I can actually glorify God just by losing weight!

My diet is only as big a deal as I make it!

I would rather be spirit filled instead of calorie filled!

I need Jesus to save me from me!

My diet is an all-or-nothing proposition!

Better to have peace of mind than a piece of cake!

When the fat won't go away, take a moment then to pray!

I may be weak, but I'm strong enough to call on God's help!

Even when I give in, I'm still a good person.

I'm never so tempted to cheat as when I'm alone!

I want to care for others as much as
I care about myself!

I'd better watch what I eat as closely
as God watches me!

I am making myself fit for life!

I will burn up calories in the fire of the Holy Spirit!

I hope I can lose my weight without losing my sensitivity toward others!

My willpower comes from the strongest power source around!

What I lack in confidence, I make up for with faith!

What I *want* to eat and what I *need* to eat are two different things!

True power is the ability to say no!

Sharing the load of dieting makes the burden light!

"More" brought about my distress;
help me Lord, to live by "less!"

There's much more to life than lunch!

The only thing God will let down is my weight!

Hunger makes me weak; losing weight makes me strong!

I don't think God will help me lose weight; I know it!

With each pound I drop, I move faster toward my goal!

I'm glad that I'm a loser ... of weight!

Too much doubt rules weight loss out!

I'm never too heavy for God to pick up!

I'm stronger than my stomach gives me credit for being!

Strength comes from unexpected places when our own gives out!

With God's help, time heals the wounds of unkind words.

Let me lose not only weight, but also false pride!

I am a marvelous creation of God, worth taking care of!

My diet will not become a burden
to anyone else!

Giving up a little at a time will keep me from giving up altogether!

It is more important to be strong of heart than strong of body!

During my diet, I'll smile even when I feel like crying!

I have more than I need, and I don't really need much of what I want.

God, save me from an appetite seldom satisfied!

I'm going to prove that there's more
to me than my weight!

Let your praises to God be louder
than the grumblings of your stomach!

I want others to see me like they've never seen me before!

I'm looking for little victories to keep me dieting!

I may fall back time and again, but I'm heading in the right direction!

In my mind I see a whole new me!

Life is a gift from God that I have no
right to abuse!

When it comes to weight, I won't kid myself!

My diet affects more than just my body; it affects my heart and mind, as well!

It's always a good idea to do what is pleasing to God!

God will send strength through family and friends!

On days when I can't help myself,
maybe I can help others!

I hope my conscience is stronger than my appetite!

My diet will end, but the lessons learned from it will last a lifetime!

God makes the joy greater than any amount of sacrifice!

I wish my heart could teach my mouth to say "no!"

Make my diet important enough to me to keep me from temptation!

I'd rather be overjoyed than overweight!

The lightness of my body is due to the light of Christ!

With God's help I will lose weight, lose hate, and lose my desire to denigrate!